JOHNNY ALLELUIA

JOHNNY
ALLELUIA

POEMS BY

CHARLES CAUSLEY

RUPERT HART-DAVIS
SOHO SQUARE LONDON
1961

© Charles Causley 1961

Printed by The Sidney Press Ltd., Bedford

TO
MY MOTHER AND FATHER
WITH LOVE

CONTENTS

ACKNOWLEDGEMENTS

The title poem, and others in this collection, first appeared in *The Listener*. Acknowledgements and thanks are also due to the editors of the following publications: in Great Britain, *The London Magazine, New Statesman, Outposts, The Tablet, Time & Tide, A Partridge in a Pear Tree, The Bryanston Miscellany, T. S. Eliot: A Symposium for his Seventieth Birthday, 45–60, The Guinness Book of Poetry 1957/1958 and 1958/ 1959, New Poems 1958 and 1961, The Saturday Book, The Compleat Imbiber*; in the United States of America, *Harper's Bazaar, Ladies' Home Journal, The Transatlantic Review*; and to the Third Programme of the B.B.C.

JOHNNY
ALLELUIA

INNOCENT'S SONG

Who's that knocking on the window,
Who's that standing at the door,
What are all those presents
Lying on the kitchen floor?

Who is the smiling stranger
With hair as white as gin,
What is he doing with the children
And who could have let him in?

Why has he rubies on his fingers,
A cold, cold crown on his head,
Why, when he caws his carol,
Does the salty snow run red?

Why does he ferry my fireside
As a spider on a thread,
His fingers made of fuses
And his tongue of gingerbread?

Why does the world before him
Melt in a million suns,
Why do his yellow, yearning eyes
Burn like saffron buns?

Watch where he comes walking
Out of the Christmas flame,
Dancing, double-talking:

Herod is his name.

PRINZ EUGEN

Prinz Eugen walked on the castle wall,
His eye was long and his leg was tall.
'Do you not fear, Prince,' I said, 'you will fall?'
Never, he answered. *Never at all.*

'Gold is your head and gold your groin,
Your nose is as neat as a Roman coin.
The spin of your skin has never a join!'

Look, said the Prince, *at my lip and my loin.*
Look at the silver that springs from my thumb,
Look for the brown blood that never will come.
Teach my beached heart the soft speech of the drum,
Feather with words the straw birds as they hum.
On my cold castle the strict sea knocks,
Butters his blade on the rim of the rocks.
Do you not hear how his ticking tongue mocks,
Slits every second and keel-hauls the clocks?

'Prince, but your gilt-edged eyebrow curls,
You stop your sentences up with pearls.
What will you do with all the girls
When love his lamp-black flag unfurls?
And Prince, your platinum fingers play
Over the maps and far away.
Are you not lord of all you survey?'
Then I am blind, I heard him say.

'Bright is your bed as the sailing shore,
Its posters up to the ceiling soar.
The servants stand at your dazzling door
To strip your senses to the core.
White is the light at your driven head,
Your body of corn stands straight as bread.
Why is your beating breast unfed?
Is it because you are dead, are dead?'

Envy me not this cloth of clay
That dries to dust all through the day.
Hurtle your heart on the pouring bay,
Answered Prinz Eugen, and limped away.

A VISIT TO VAN GOGH
at the Asylum of Saint-Paul-du-Mausolée

The French bus halts on the Plateau of Antiques
Unloads its cargo on the sweating square,
The Arch of Glanum, cut with vines and captives,
Explodes in triumph on the Roman air.
In their mausolée, Caius and young Lucius
Watch the white mountain from their cage of bone
And the shot city, untongued by disaster,
Burns on the blue a hundred flames of stone.

Wearing the straw hat of the sun, the mad sun
I strolled the staring sulphur flowers by.
Paint streamed like Christ's blood in the firmament.
Stone-pine and cypress crucified the sky.
An exclamation of black baking olives
Silenced the stunning light. I pulled the bell.
You are, she seemed to say who made an answer,
Seventy years late. Enter. We know you well.

Down the dead path the whining of a fountain.
Tin voices overhead of birds, bells, clocks.
The awful silence of the pot geranium
At God knows what wrecks on these flowers, these rocks.
In the drowned cloister the white wading rose tree
Wrote on the water's throat its gift of gall,
Lanced with thorn the torn air, the enormous answer
To the cold question of the asylum wall.

A priest with shilling hair, boots and a cycle
Clumped past to benediction, eyes away.
The roof has fallen on the painter's studio.
Is out of bounds. To come another day.
Another day? I crossed, I said, a lifetime
To hold this vine, these olives in my hand.
He hurried with pure pom-faced nuns. *The service*
Must take its usual course, you understand?

You wish to see him? The old woman pointed:
A dusted field-path stitched with oil and vines.
I walked into the golden gape of summer.
The mountain slept, showed prehistoric spines.
Turning, I met the long glare of the madhouse,
A single unbarred stare, a square eye.
See, he is here! It was the old woman, waving
At mountain, meadow, air and tree and sky.

I saw, that storied summer at the bus stop
Under basilicas of birds, a marble eye
Flash from the fettered arch, the trim mausolée
Slung, hard as history, on the heavy sky.
The man ignored, I said, your obvious story.
Did you remark him as he passed you by?
On their proud pillar, Lucius and young Caius
Combed their stone hair, laughed, and made no reply.

MOTHER, GET UP, UNBAR THE DOOR

Mother, get up, unbar the door,
Throw wide the window-pane,
I see a man stand all covered in sand
Outside in Vicarage Lane.

His body is shot with seventy stars,
His face is cold as Cain,
His coat is a crust of desert dust
And he comes from Alamein.

He has not felt the flaking frost,
He has not felt the rain,
And not one blow of the burning snow
Since the night that he was slain.

O mother, in your husband's arms
Too long now you have lain,
Rise up, my dear, your true-love's here
Upon the peaceful plain.

Though, mother, on your broken brow
Forty long years are lain,
The soldier they slew at twenty-two
Never a one does gain.

I will unlock the fine front-door
And snap the silver chain,
And meek as milk in my skin of silk
I'll ease him of his pain.

My breast has been for years eighteen
As white as Charles's wain,
But now I'm had by a soldier lad
Whistling *Lili Marlene*.

Farewell to Jack, farewell to Jim,
And farewell Mary Jane,
Farewell the good green sisterhood
Knitting at purl and plain.

Go wash the water from your eye,
The bullet from your brain.
I'm drowned as a dove in the tunnel of love
And I'll never come home again.

EMBLEMS OF THE PASSION

Here, you said, the voice well-bred
Carried in that classic head,
Unremarking, as your fashion,
That the slipping sky was ashen,
Are the Emblems of the Passion.

Overhead a heeling bird
Struck on the split sky the word,
But I do not think you heard
As the blood of the last sun
On the wounded water spun.

Safe beneath a shooting spire
Here you waded the green wire
Of the graveyard's fallen fire,
Dreams, desires, as fish asleep
In the silence of its deep.

On the raging wood, unread
Histories of the hanged, the dead
Searched the cyphers of my head:
Soldier, seamless robe on rail,
Hyssop, hammer, crown and nail.

From the forest of my fears
Thirty-coined, a tree of tears
Flowered on the sour, slab floor
By the high, the holy door
Of death's strict and silent shore.

Hand with scourges, hand with spear,
Lantern, ladder, cross and gear,
Cock on pillar. Chaste and clear
God's trapping tongue : *Consider this*
Head of Judas, and the kiss.

Underneath that seamless sky
Stripped, I met your startled eye
Saw your sweating lip, and I
Whose face was Judas, felt you start
At the rivers of the heart.

CRISTO DE BRISTOL

*The 'Cristo de Bristol' is an articulated figure of Christ
used for the Easter Sepulchre and carried through the
streets of a fishing village of northern Spain during the
Holy Week processions. It is said to have been dredged
from the Avon by a Spanish sea-captain, who brought
the figure to his home port.*

I am the Bristol Christ,
That waking man who won
With hands of wire the Easter fire
Out of the Biscay sun.
Cast in my coat of lights
Upon the poking tide
A seaman with a snare of stars
Hauled me to his side.

Swim on, Captain Jesus,
Wherever you may wish.
Write on the wicked water
The message of the fish.
Heal in the holy river
Your five and fingered scars,
Turn like a tree about the sea
Your skeleton of spars.

I stepped from off the ocean
Upon the sea-struck shore,
I laid me down my cruel crown
Before my father's door.
I carried him that kingdom
I set beneath my skin
That he might seal the sorrow
Of all the world within.

Now springs upon your shipmast
The burning bush of day,
From your shot side the breathing tide
Wears the black grave away.
Bless with your fan of fingers
These hands, this heart, these eyes,
And lift my love and fishes
Perfect, to paradise.

O BILLY, DO YOU HEAR THAT BELL?

O Billy, do you hear that bell
  Speaking from the spire?
Has Willie Fell gone down the well
  Or is it *Fire, fire?*
And do you see a cinder star
  Sizzling in the sky,
And crazy Kings with burning wings
  Learning how to fly?

O sister, soft as any shawl
  The sharp snow winds the wire,
Pale as a pall the cattle trawl
  Their breath about the byre.
Now in the rare and eating air
  The bird chinks on the thorn,
And slowly through the holy blue
  The shepherd hauls his horn.

O father, is that cruel cry
  Coming from the mire
A Wise Man lost in the world's frost
  Or is it only Squire?
And when the alleluia boys
  Drum their December din,
Why do you call the constable
  That he may lock them in?

O mother, who will find the flock
  And harness up the shire,
And who will lock the weather-clock
  If winter does not tire,
And who will ship a farthing dip
  Upon the drifting day,
And seize a spark from heaven's dark
  To burn the night away?

O Billy, will you wag the word
  From off your freezing tongue,
Nor hire the hearse or district nurse
  Because I am so young?
And shall we push the business on
  And do the best we can
To cut free from the Christmas tree
  The hanging, holy man?

EARLY IN THE MORNING

Early in the morning
The water hits the rocks,
The birds are making noises
Like old alarum clocks,
The soldier on the skyline
Fires a golden gun
And over the back of the chimney-stack
Explodes the silent sun.

Johnny packs his parcel
And wanders off to war,
His body blond as butter
But he don't know what it's for.
They'll post it all in pieces
Straight to City Hall
As I sleep in my skin with a tender twin
Under the waterfall.

Wheeling with the weather
He curls the cut-glass air,
The girls won't take no notice
But all the cattle stare.
In a forge of feathers
He swarms into the sea
And lights his head about the bed
Of my true-love and me.

Say goodbye to your uncle,
His pockets are built of brass,
Wherever you find his footmarks
There never grows no grass.
Whether you fly your fortune
Finer than a flea
Or march the map or guard the gap
It's all the same to me.

I'll love her in the morning
I'll love her in the night
I'll love her till the sun shines black
And the walking stars are white
My tongue is made of flowers
My breath is made of milk
My hip and thigh are made of rye
And my hand is made of silk.

Beneath my winter window
That once was warm as wheat
I see the sprigs of summer
Starving in the sleet,
And every wasting white-boy
His heart as cold as a crow
In the sound of the skies like the shepherd lies
And pulls up the snow.

THE VOYAGE OF THE *SAINTES-MARIES*

I, the sick seaman from the unspoken north
Firing my vessel on the sacred strand
Mark now how Lazarus with unbandaged breath
Clasps my cold fingers with a warm, clay hand,
Casts his killed eye upon the breaking bay
Where in their bibled boat the Maries stand
Pouring a plaster blessing on the day
As he winds his white ship of saints to land.

This barque, they said, built of the Jesus tree,
Launched by twin thieves and held by holy nails,
We now deliver from the dying sea,
Dry in the diving sky its shroud of sails.
Descending from the water's written stair
Marie Salomé, at the struck ship's fore
Marie Jacobé, branched with burning hair
Passed without print upon the stealing shore.

Where the slit sea-grass guts the shoals of air
We build our church, they said, upon this sand.
On each stone, stuck to perfect stone with prayer,
The river rubs with fifty-fingered hand.
With ropes of water and with ropes of light
We hoist these syllables of sticks, of spars
As in the silence of the shifting night
Walks the mad moon its cemetery of stars

In the blacked church before the noise of candles
I see the saints in springs of fire sown,
Read with a risen eye the wrist that handles
The starting water as if it were stone,
And with the reliquaries of the sun
In architraves of air your talking bone
Sets with sharp flowers for flames. You speak of one
Who murdered death and from the grave has flown.

Now from your trap of towers burst the bell
With turning tongue upon the travelled sky.
Before the fevers of your blazing cell
Fishermen, cowboys, shipwrecked lovers lie.
August goddesses, on your sleep of stone
I see the paint's blood, the burned words of wire,
The sawdust tears upon the city sown,
But at your feet the fire, the holy fire.

SONNET TO THE HOLY VINE

On the report of an oppressed Spanish donkey who, after drinking eighteen pints of wine, turned on his persecutors and won a new independence.

Here sleeps Don Diego, *burro*, of this city,
The sticks of Jesus strapped upon his spine,
Who burned away his pack of pain and pity
In fires of garnet gathered from the vine.
Through the white winter and the summer shine
He laboured for the kingdom of the ape
Until he wrote his talking throat with wine
And grasped eternity within the grape.
Before Don Diego, Phoebus-tongued with flares,
Doctor, priest, lawyer, soldier of the line,
Rose from their naked knees with pitching prayers
And bore his skin of war to this shrine
Where he now lies beneath the throbbing thorn
And in three days will rise, like man, reborn.

MASTER AND PUPIL
(on a theme of Demetrios Capetanakis)

He shook the bandage from his snowing head,
Flooded with fire his hollow heart of stone.
It was as clear as blood, the neighbours said.
The old man had no children of his own.

When they both walked upon the sharp sea-shore,
He with his hand within the gold boy's breast,
The colours of the cock the winter wore,
The shot sun faltered in the flowing west.

We never can forget that sight, they cried.
Who would have thought of murder, the police?
It was as if, somehow, we all had spied
Some mentionable scene from Ancient Greece.

A Sunday paper printed all the facts,
Developing in paschal blood their day.
There was a front-page picture of the axe,
But all the innocence was wiped away.

No greater love has any man than this
That lays a friend's life down to save his own,
They murmur, sealing with a loving kiss
The cracked, cold body in its suit of stone.

He never spilt an atom of regret,
They sigh. *The boy shows no respect for death*,
As on the striking day he hangs his debt,
Stands on the hour and sucks a last, strapped breath.

AT GRANTCHESTER

Bank Holiday. A sky of guns. The river
Slopping black silver on the level stair.
A war-memorial that aims for ever
Its stopped, stone barrel on the enormous air.

A hoisted church, its cone of silence stilling
The conversations of the crow, the kite.
A coasting chimney-stack, advancing, filling
With smoking blossom the lean orchard light.

The verse, I am assured, has long ceased ticking
Though the immortal clock strikes ten to three,
The fencing wasp fights for its usual picking
And tongues of honey hang from every tree.

The swilling sea with its unvarying thunder
Searches the secret face of famous stone.
On the thrown wind blown words like hurt birds wander
That from the maimed, the murdered mouth have flown.

DOWN BY THE RIVERSIDE
(*for the seventieth birthday of T. S. Eliot*)

Down by the riverside the grass grows deep,
Seventy branches tiger-stripe my sheep,
And where the Tamar turns her watery fan
I search its city for the pavement-man.

    At Launceston in the year that I was born
    The ragged poppies ran around the corn
    And red October blew her bloody gale
    About the flooded field of Passchendaele.

I saw a man with sherbet in his hair
Rope camels to the coast of Russell Square
And seizing sea-coals from his burning hat
(God and the world knows what he saw in that!)
Print on the shaken shore with perfect hand
Poems like oak trees in a wasted land
And thresh with thunder from the sounding sky
The beating echo of a battle cry.

    Then with cats, angels, saints, thugs, for the dark
    Take love, the last unconfidential clerk,
    That flames like flowers might burn above his bed
    As the white elder blossom at my head.

Now summer, and this wandering humble, hums
On the gold air epithalamiums
I and my true-love at the river's rim
These words upon the salmon-waters swim
And launch a laurel for his birthday brow—
Hoping it finds him as it leaves us now.

HEALING A LUNATIC BOY

Trees turned and talked to me,
Tigers sang,
Houses put on leaves,
Water rang.
Flew in, flew out
On my tongue's thread
A speech of birds
From my hurt head.

At my fine loin
Fire and cloud kissed,
Rummaged the green bone
Beneath my wrist.
I saw a sentence
Of fern and tare
Write with loud light
The mineral air.

On a stopped morning
The city spoke,
In my rich mouth
Oceans broke.
No more on the spun shore
I walked unfed.
I drank the sweet sea,
Stones were bread.

Then came the healer
Grave as grass,
His hair of water
And hands of glass.
I watched at his tongue
The white words eat,
In death, dismounted
At his stabbed feet.

Now river is river
And tree is tree,
My house stands still
As the northern sea.
On my hundred of parables
I heard him pray,
Seize my smashed world,
Wrap it away.

Now the pebble is sour,
The birds beat high,
The fern is silent,
The river dry.
A seething summer
Burned to bone
Feeds at my mouth
But finds a stone.

C

ACTAEON AND ARTEMIS

Young Actaeon, leaning on the lake of leaves,
Feeding his fallow leg with forest air,
Observes his hounds, where the rapt fountain grieves,
Belling in accents of antique despair.

The Furies, clouding in the classic sky,
Unnoticed by our hero, chalk his slate.
He checks each pad, each dumb distempered eye.
Puts it all down to something that they ate.

And from the smoking waters of the stream
Artemis rises in her skin of grape,
Covers her breasts, emits a civil scream,
Conceives of no alternative but rape.

The young man, innocent as all that blue,
Ponders, still vaguely, on those violent sounds.
Artemis, armed, fails to accept the view
That Actaeon's thoughts could merely be of hounds.

Of course, her casual magic never fails.
Actaeon, stag-struck, stands defenceless, mute,
As ticking their tin metronomes of tails
His idiot hounds now hurtle in pursuit.

With trailing tongues they wipe the wandered light,
Beat down the bush of horns. The white wounds blaze.
Then, with milled eyes, they take to marble flight
Eager, as usual, for their master's praise.

He was as free as flesh, as blood, from blame.
He thought of hounds, of hunting, Chiron said.
Not to have gazed is even greater shame,
Artemis cried, and turned her famous head.

MISS ELLIOTT

Little Miss Elliott died in the dark
At ninety-five, Victoria Park.

I saw as I strolled in the ivory air
The Prince of Darkness stand on her stair,

Scaled in sharp black from cap to toe,
About him his soldiers swarming like snow,

Armed with all hell and bladed with light,
Banners and torches and thunderbolts bright,

War-horses hammering holes in the sky,
Waiting for little Miss Elliott to die.

And as Miss Elliott her last, lean breath furled
Out of the vertical midnight they hurled,

Drawing their swords from the corpse of the sun,
A million warriors falling on one.

But, as they slung down the shattering air,
Little Miss Elliott was no longer there :

I saw, as they sank with the sound of the swan,
Little Miss Elliott had gone, gone, gone.

FOR AN EX-FAR EAST PRISONER OF WAR

I am that man with helmet made of thorn
Who wandered naked in the desert place,
Wept, with the sweating sky, that I was born
And wore disaster in my winter face.

I am that man who asked no hate, nor pity.
I am that man, five-wounded, on the tree.
I am that man, walking his native city,
Hears his dead comrade cry, *Remember me!*

I am that man whose brow with blood was wet,
Returned, as Lazarus, from the dead to live.
I am that man, long-counselled to forget,
Facing a fearful victory, to forgive :

And seizing these two words, with the sharp sun
Beat them, like sword and ploughshare, into one.

MY FRIEND MALONEY

My friend Maloney, eighteen,
　　Swears like a sentry,
Got into trouble two years back
　　With the local gentry.

Parson and squire's sons
　　Informed a copper.
The magistrate took one look at Maloney,
　　Fixed him proper.

Talked of the crime of youth,
　　The innocent victim.
Maloney never said a blind word
　　To contradict him.

Maloney of Gun Street,
　　Back of the Nuclear Mission,
Son of the town whore,
　　Blamed television.

Justice, as usual, triumphed.
　　Everyone felt fine.
Things went deader.
　　Maloney went up the line.

Maloney learned one lesson :
　　Never play the fool
With the products of especially a minor
　　Public school.

Maloney lost a thing or two
　　At that institution.
First shirt, second innocence,
　　The old irresolution.

Found himself a girl-friend,
   Sharp suit, sharp collars.
Maloney on a moped,
   Pants full of dollars.

College boys on the corner
   In striped, strait blazers
Look at old Maloney,
   Eyes like razors.

You don't need talent, says Maloney.
   You don't need looks.
All I got you got, fellers.
   You can keep your thick books.

Parson got religion,
   Squire, in the end, the same.
The magistrate went over the wall.
   Life, said Maloney, 's a game.

Consider then the case of Maloney,
   College boys, parson, squire, beak.
Who was the victor and who was the victim?
   Speak.

THE BALLAD OF BILLY OF NOSEY BENT
or HOW TO MAKE A POET

When I was born at Nosey Bent
    They watched the windows and raised the rent
They hung out my parents' wedding line
    To see if I'd paid my nine-month fine
And when they found I'd overspent
    They said my father was impotent.

When I went out on the patch to play
    The village children ran away
Salt was my hair as the sea-bay sand
    And I'd seven fingers on each hand
My face was white as the workhouse wall
    And I wore my head like a cannon-ball.

While the children danced all over the hill
    I cut the corn with Looney Lil
She didn't know what was three times seven
    But she unscrewed her eyes and showed me heaven
I pillowed my head on her wounded breast
    And the sun baled out in the bleeding west.

When the leaf lay light on the sycamore stem
    They tried to send me to Bethlehem
The King of Passion, the Queen of Pain
    Danced in their tower and lanced my brain
Trapped my tongue in a silver bit
    That I might neither speak nor spit.

They said I would neither sing nor say
    But young Prince Hamlet came my way
And took me to his house to dine
    On salads of lilies and ballads of wine
Till I cast my cloak on the curling snow
    Where the naked neighbours of Nosey go.

The Count of Nosey has a coat of mail
   But I fly feathered like the nightingale
Cold is my cage as death's bright dart
   But my walls stand soft as a poor man's heart
Three Wise Men wait at my garden gate
   My crown is crooked, but my jacket is strait.

THREE GIPSIES

Three gipsies stood at my drifted door,
One was rich and one was poor
And one had the face of a blackamoor.

Out of the murdering moor they came,
One was leaping, two were lame,
And each called out my naked name.

'Is there a baby that wants within
A penny of brass and a crown of tin
And a fire of spice for original sin?

'Hold him high at the window wide
That we may beg for him a Bride
From the circling star that swings outside.'

'Rise up, rise up, you gipsies three
Your baskets of willow and rush I see
And the third that is made of the Judas tree.

'No boy is born in my bed this day
Where the icicle fires her freezing ray,
For my love has risen and run away.

'So fare you well, Egyptians three,
Who bow and bring to me the key
From the cells of sin to set us free.'

Out of the million-angeled sky
As gold as the hairs of my head and thigh
I heard a new-born baby cry.

'Come back, come back, you gipsies three
And put your packs by my Christmas tree
For it is my son's nativity!'

Over the marble meadow and plain
The gipsies rode by the river's skein
And never more did they come again.

I set a star in the window tall,
The bread and wine in my waiting hall
And a heap of hay in the mangers all,

But the gipsies three with their gifts were gone,
And where the host of heaven had shone
The lunatic moon burned on, burned on.

BIBLE STORY

In August, when the air of love was peeled,
I saw a burning boy upon the bed,
Shut a green shade against the harvest field
And held one shaking hand behind his head.

Stripped of his skin of breath, his heart untied,
I searched his threaded throat of serpentine,
And lying on the pallet at his side
I drew his beaten breast of milk to mine.

In this stone shell I poured such seas of prayer
His sailing soul was driven down from heaven,
His prodigal parents on the ringing stair
Heard, as the sun struck six, the boy sneeze seven,

And as he wandered, innocent, from my prison
Cried, *Hail, Elisha, for our son is risen*!

THE BALLAD OF CHARLOTTE DYMOND

*Charlotte Dymond, a domestic servant aged eighteen, was
murdered near Rowtor Ford on Bodmin Moor on Sunday,
14th April, 1844, by her young man: a crippled farm-hand,
Matthew Weeks, aged twenty-two. A stone marks the spot.*

It was a Sunday evening
　　And in the April rain
That Charlotte went from our house
　　And never came home again.

Her shawl of diamond redcloth,
　　She wore a yellow gown,
She carried the green gauze handkerchief
　　She bought in Bodmin town.

About her throat her necklace
　　And in her purse her pay:
The four silver shillings
　　She had at Lady Day.

In her purse four shillings
　　And in her purse her pride
As she walked out one evening
　　Her lover at her side.

Out beyond the marshes
　　Where the cattle stand,
With her crippled lover
　　Limping at her hand.

Charlotte walked with Matthew
　　Through the Sunday mist,
Never saw the razor
　　Waiting at his wrist.

Charlotte she was gentle
   But they found her in the flood
Her Sunday beads among the reeds
   Beaming with her blood.

Matthew, where is Charlotte,
   And wherefore has she flown?
For you walked out together
   And now are come alone.

Why do you not answer,
   Stand silent as a tree,
Your Sunday worsted stockings
   All muddied to the knee?

Why do you mend your breast-pleat
   With a rusty needle's thread
And fall with fears and silent tears
   Upon your single bed?

Why do you sit so sadly
   Your face the colour of clay
And with a green gauze handkerchief
   Wipe the sour sweat away?

Has she gone to Blisland
   To seek an easier place,
And is that why your eye won't dry
   And blinds your bleaching face?

'Take me home!' cried Charlotte,
   'I lie here in the pit!
A red rock rests upon my breasts
   And my naked neck is split!'

45

Her skin was soft as sable,
    Her eyes were wide as day,
Her hair was blacker than the bog
    That licked her life away.

Her cheeks were made of honey,
    Her throat was made of flame
Where all around the razor
    Had written its red name.

As Matthew turned at Plymouth
    About the tilting Hoe,
The cold and cunning Constable
    Up to him did go:

'I've come to take you, Matthew,
    Unto the Magistrate's door.
Come quiet now, you pretty poor boy,
    And you must know what for.'

'She is as pure,' cried Matthew,
    'As is the early dew,
Her only stain it is the pain
    That round her neck I drew!

She is as guiltless as the day
    She sprang forth from her mother.
The only sin upon her skin
    Is that she loved another.'

They took him off to Bodmin,
    They pulled the prison bell,
They sent him smartly up to Heaven
    And dropped him down to Hell.

All through the granite kingdom
    And on its travelling airs
Ask which of these two lovers
    The most deserves your prayers.

And your steel heart search, Stranger,
    That you may pause and pray
For lovers who come not to bed
    Upon their wedding day,

But lie upon the moorland
    Where stands the sacred snow
Above the breathing river,
    And the salt sea-winds go.

Lying within my island, rung by birds,
Books on the waving wall, sheets bright as bread,
The moon, fast in a foliage of words
Turning its wheel of blades above my head,

I see the night, her cataract of tides
Strike with black sounds the citadel of bone,
And in the scarlet river of my side
Swim the great stars, unwritten and alone.

Now seas of silence drift the dropping air
My bathed blood, calm beneath the sailing skin
Coasts the locked colonies of quiet, where
The swivelled sun burns black upon its pin.

With the salt ceremonies of the sea
A fabled peace breaks on the body's shore,
Storms fall as flowers from the ravished tree
Safe in my myth of arms for evermore.

Out of the wreathing rivers of the east
A scream rips wide my eyes, freezes my hair,
Whether of man or child or bird or beast
I, with the raging stars, am unaware.

Who gave, I start, that caught, that climbing call
And drags with death the water's moving mile?
The appalling seas beyond the harbour wall
Throw up their white and waiting hands, and smile.

CHRIST AT THE CHEESEWRING*

As I walked on the wicked moor
Where seven smashed stones lie
I met a man with a skin of tan
And an emerald in his eye.

All naked was his burning back
And naked was his thigh,
His only cloak it was the smoke
Out of the failing sky.

O loudly did he nail my name
Upon the mine-stacks three
And louder rose the ragged crows
That sail above the sea.

> *O will you drink my body deep*
> *And wash my five wounds dry*
> *That shot with snow now gravely grow*
> *As scarlet as the sky?*

> *All down, he said, the drowning day*
> *And down the damaged sky*
> *God's naked son his fingers won*
> *About my thieving eye,*

> *And like a bough about my brow*
> *Planted a hand of horn*
> *That men may see mirrored in me*
> *The image of the thorn.*

I see no badge upon your brow
I drink no five wounds dry
I see no thief wrecked on the reef
Where seven smashed stones lie.

* *A granite cairn, thirty feet high, at the south-east corner*
of Bodmin Moor in Cornwall

Above the stone, above the sun,
Above the swinging sky
The King of Heaven the days seven
Is hanging out to die!

Softly he touched my turning head
And softly touched my side
And blessed with bread the waters red
That on the sea-bay slide.

I saw him climb the canvas sun
The strapped world to untie,
On its sharp strand with splintered hand
The flags of heaven fly.

I scattered in a sand of stars
His hand, his lip, his thigh,
I plucked the thorn that he had worn
Above his beating eye.

And on the land where seven stones stand
He stretched his hand to me
And on my brow of staring snow
Printed a gallows-tree.

CHILD'S SONG

Christopher Beer
Used to live here,
Where the white water
Winds over the weir,
Close to the claw
Of the pawing sea,
Under the spear
Of a cypress tree.

Never a nightingale
Rings on the bough,
Burned is the orchard
And broken the plough.
Out of the orient
Light like a lash
Severed the sky
And the river ran ash.

Over the valley
Dawdled the fire
Swallowing city
Steeple and spire,
All the proud people
Nowhere to hide
Kindling flowers
Of flame as they died.

Nobody passes
Nor sheds a salt tear,
No-one wears mourning
For Christopher Beer:
Free as the fountain,
Green as a gun,
Rich as the rainbow
And blind as the sun.

THREE MASTS

Three masts has the thrusting ship,
Three masts will she wear
When she like Christ our Saviour
Walks on the watery stair.

One stands at the fore
To meet the weather wild
As He who once in winter
Was a little child.

One grows after
From step to the sky
For He who once was keel-hauled
And hung up to die.

One stands amidships
Between fore and mizzen
Pointing to paradise
For He who is risen.

Three masts will grow on the green ship
Before she quits the quay,
For Father, Son, and Holy Ghost:
Blessed Trinity.

THE TEMPTATION OF SAINT DUNSTAN

Blessed Saint Dunstan, master of iron, of arts,
Forger, in fired air, of cross and vial,
Fold now your file of fingers at my trial
Of winter words as the long light departs.

At Candlemas you from the black womb came,
All tapers, save your marvellous mother's, dimmed
Yet leaping from the naked legs you trimmed
Earth's lantern from her unextinguished flame.

Now tonsured, blessed by Elphegus the Bald,
Young Edwi with your poulticed prayers you scald—
That King who inconsiderately lay
With the wreathed harlot on his crowning day.

And when, with tongue of knives, the monks expelling
You on the cautious air your colours telling
Bade Woman and the apple-tree take heed
The figure on the crucifix agreed.

But as you stood within the forge's smoke
Robed in the reverent attitudes of day,
There stepped from the sly, severed air of May
A naked girl with hair her only cloak.

Two bearded devils rested at her brow,
Two devils rested at her ruined eyes,
Two rested at her breast of braided snow,
One where her hand discreetly hid her thighs.

The Blessed Saint, calm as the composed sun,
Saw in that fatal frame the Evil One;
Replaced, with prayer, her seven shells of clothes
And seized with his swift tongs her naked nose.

O but the Evil One with dreadful yells
Now sprang, with smoking skin, to Tunbridge Wells
And drove its nose out of the burning air
Into the chalybeaten waters there.

While in his house of forges Dunstan lay,
Hammered Christ's kingdom from the heavy clay,
Wrote, chastised, painted, walked with God, and died
In the white odours of Ascensiontide.

And still, from the sure sky, as seasons flow
I watch, with Dunstan, the frail flowers of snow,
My cell-door open on my shirt of skin
That all who wish may knock and enter in.

At my tall table, paper virgin-bright,
A sand of silence, sea-lantern alight
That she may land from that shut, sacred ark
With whitsun days of words upon my dark.

O may she come upon this noonday clear,
Unfreeze the drifted heart! See, I have here
The ink's blood, iron pen, the forge well fired,
And the sharp tongs that may not be required.

NOW

Now that you leave me for that other friend,
Rich as the rubbed sun, elegant of eye,
Who watched, in lost light, your five fortunes end
And wears the weapons of the wasted sky,

Often, I say, I saw him at your gate,
Noted well how he passed the time of day,
Gazed, with bright greed, at your young man's estate
And how, in fear, I looked the other way.

For we had met, this thief and I, before
On terrible seas, at the spoiled city's heart,
And when I saw him standing at your door
Nothing, I knew, could put you now apart.

O with sly promises he stroked the air,
Struck, on the coin of day, his gospel face.
I saw you turn, touch his hand, unaware
Of his thorned kiss or of his grave embrace.

GUY FAWKES' DAY

I am the caught, the cooked, the candled man
With flames for fingers and whose thin eyes fountain,
I send on the stiff air my shooting stare
And at my shoulder bear the burning mountain.

I open on the dark my wound of speeches,
With stabs, with stars its seven last words wear,
My tongue of torches with the salamander
Breeds conversaziones of despair.

Milled in the minted light my skin of silver
Now curls, now kindles on the thicket's bone,
And fired with flesh in sepulchres of slumber
Walks the white night with sparks and showers sown.

At my fixed feet soldiers my coat of carbon
Slit with the speared sky. Their sacked eyes scan
My mask of medals. In bright mirrors of breath
Our faces fuse in death. My name is man.

SAILORS ASLEEP IN A CINEMA

On shores of celluloid the sailors lie,
Caps piled in slices as life's bread and clay,
Dreaming of shirts and steaks, the polished thigh,
And sleep the giant actor's wars away.

One with pale throat thrown back and drifting limb
As for the naked dagger bares his breath;
Head on wrung hands or at an oppoe's arm, they swim
In attitudes of innocence or death.

Or on a primitive Italian sea
They glide within the grove of spinning smoke,
Stunned, as Christ's seamen in Gethsemane,
The darkness dragged about them like a cloak.

O in such easy postures of defeat
My comrades keep their violent vigils still,
Wear in salt air the water's weather-sheet
And stir beneath the ocean's heavy hill.

Ice tries the trim, the tropic air for size.
The burst sun, scarred with burning birds, is gone.
Before our driven and disregarding eyes
Images sweat. The winding world roars on.

JOHNNY ALLELUIA

Johnny Alleluia
  In a seven-year cell
Watched the walking morning
  Didn't feel well,
Stretched for a string
  Of the leaping light,
Nailed it to his neck-bone
  Tacked it tight.

Up went Johnny
  In the blue, bold air,
You should have seen
  The screws all stare.
Johnny? they said,
  More lives than a cat.
Never should have thought he'd done
  A thing like that.

Johnny was a tinker
  Tramped to the fair,
His kettles as bright
  As his tinplate hair.
With his tongue of chicken
  And his breast of ham
Johnny didn't give
  A tinker's damn.

It was good old Johnny,
  And Johnny here's the key,
And Johnny put your hand
  Where it shouldn't be.
O the girls all laughed
  And the boys didn't care
When Johnny came up
  Their kitchen stair.

But what is this blade
  And what is this stone,
And why don't you take
  A wife of your own?
Why do you wear
  Your breeches so tight,
And what is this drum
  Of dynamite?

I sharpen my knife
  On the winding stone
To cut me an apple
  From the branch of bone.
My pants so tight
  Keep my legs apart,
And I blast with powder
  The human heart.

Is this a bunch
  Of skeleton keys,
And what is this wax
  Under your chemise?
Why are your eyes
  So clear, my son,
And you still under
  Twenty-one?

Under my shirt
  My keys and my wax
Unlock the body
  And silence the cracks.
I hear in my heart
  The gold blood gad
As it did in the days
  When Adam was a lad.

It was Now then, Johnny,
   And Johnny take care,
For boys like you
   There's nothing to spare.
In the lake of love
   You're sure to drown,
You can't walk on water
   In this town.

You must keep your fingers
   To yourself
And your lollipop eye
   From another man's shelf.
And Johnny don't take
   Too long a pull
At all things bright
   And beautiful.

They shanghai'd Johnny
   In a squinting cell
With modern plumbing
   And a view of hell.
They disinfected
   His public parts
And sketched his soul
   On little charts.

So he cast off shore
   And swung to sea.
The Governor wept,
   He said, said he,
It was ever thus!
   And shook his head.

I'm damned if it was,
   Young Johnny said.

GRAVE BY THE SEA

By the crunching, Cornish sea
Walk the man and walk the lover,
Innocent as fish that fare
In the high and hooking air,
And their deaths discover.

Beneath, you said, this turning tree,
With granite eye and stare of sand,
His heart as candid as the clay,
A seaman from the stropping bay
Took to the land.

Once this calmed, crystal hand was free
And rang the changes of the heart:
Love, like his life, a world wherein
The white-worm sin wandered not in.
Death played no part.

Wreathed, and with ringing fingers he
Passed like a prince upon the day
And from its four and twenty towers
Shot with his shaft the haggard hours,
Hauled them away.

So he set from the shaken quay
His foot upon the ocean floor
And from the wanting water's teeth
The ice-faced gods above, beneath,
Spat him ashore.

Now in the speaking of the sea
He waits under this written stone,
And kneeling at his freezing frame
I scrub my eye to see his name

And read my own.